A **TRUE** BOOK

National Parks
Yosemite

AUDRA WALLACE

Children's Press®
An Imprint of Scholastic Inc.

Content Consultant

James Gramann, PhD
Professor, Department of Recreation, Park and Tourism Sciences
Texas A&M University, College Station, Texas

Library of Congress Cataloging-in-Publication Data
Names: Wallace, Audra author.
Title: Yosemite / by Audra Wallace.
Description: New York : Children's Press, An Imprint of Scholastic Inc., 2018. | Series: A true book
  | Includes bibliographical references and index.
Identifiers: LCCN 2017004665 | ISBN 9780531233955 (library binding) | ISBN 9780531240229 (pbk.)
Subjects: LCSH: Yosemite National Park (Calif.)—Juvenile literature.
Classification: LCC F868.Y6 W336 2018 | DDC 979.4/47—dc23
LC record available at https://lccn.loc.gov/2017004665

SCHOLASTIC, CHILDREN'S PRESS, A TRUE BOOK™, and associated logos are trademarks and/or registered trademarks of Scholastic Inc., 557 Broadway, New York, NY 10012.
1 2 3 4 5 6 7 8 9 10 R 27 26 25 24 23 22 21 20 19 18

Front cover (main): Yosemite Falls

Front cover (inset): Climbers resting on a portaledge on El Capitan

Back cover: A great grey owl

★ Find the Truth!

Everything you are about to read is true *except* for one of the sentences on this page.

Which one is **TRUE**?

T or F   Yosemite was the United States' first national park.

T or F   Some trees in Yosemite are more than 2,000 years old.

Find the answers in this book.

Contents

THE **BIG** TRUTH!

National Parks Field Guide: Yosemite

**The National Park
Service logo**

Yosemite in the fall

This famous photo
of Overhanging Rock
was taken in 1916.

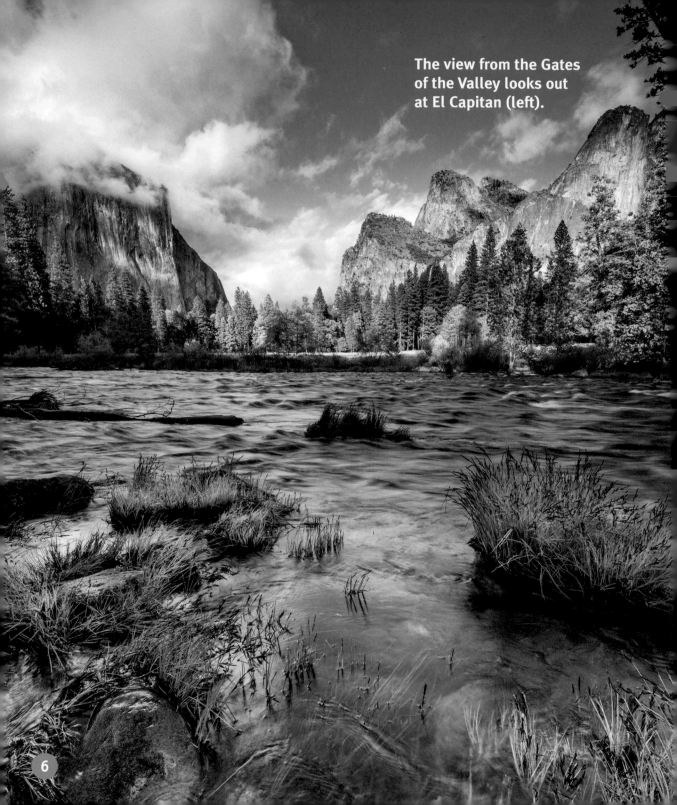

The view from the Gates of the Valley looks out at El Capitan (left).

CHAPTER 1

A Long History

Millions of years ago, rivers and **glaciers** carved through the Sierra Nevada mountains in California, forming Yosemite Valley. It is the centerpiece of Yosemite National Park. People visit the park to climb its gigantic rock formations. They trek to its roaring waterfalls. They also gaze up at its towering trees. It is a place to connect with nature, view star-filled night skies, and find adventure.

The Merced River, which flows through Yosemite Valley, is 145 miles (233 kilometers) long.

★ Yosemite National Park

The First People

Native Americans first moved into Yosemite Valley about 8,000 years ago. At this time, a group of people from the South Sierra Miwok tribe made their home there. They called themselves the Ahwahneechee. The Ahwahneechee were known as fierce warriors. Other tribes called them Yosemite. *Yosemite* is thought to come from the Miwok word *uzumati*, which means "grizzly bear."

A Timeline of Yosemite National Park

1890

Yosemite becomes a national park.

1891–1913

The Buffalo Soldiers, a segregated African American unit of the U.S. Army, help preserve Yosemite.

1907

The Yosemite Valley Railroad opens, bringing thousands of tourists to the park.

Gold Rush!

The first Europeans and white Americans arrived in Yosemite during the mid-1800s. Thousands of miners traveled through the area on their way to search for gold in California's mountains. Word spread about Yosemite's natural wonders, especially its **groves** of giant sequoia (si-KWOI-uh) trees. Soldiers from California drove native people from their homes in order to claim the area. White people settled there soon after. Tourists also came. Many were artists, writers, and photographers.

1913
The National Park Service is created to protect national parks. Cars are officially allowed to enter Yosemite, increasing park visits significantly.

1918
Yosemite's Claire Marie Hodges becomes the first female park ranger in the National Park Service.

1954
Yosemite welcomes its one-millionth visitor.

Paving the Way

Conservationists were concerned that too much human activity would harm the land. They persuaded President Abraham Lincoln to protect the area. In 1864, Lincoln signed a bill called the Yosemite Grant Act. It made Yosemite Valley and Mariposa Grove a public trust of California. That meant the state's government was responsible for maintaining the land's resources for public enjoyment. This was the first time in U.S. history that land had been protected by a state in this way.

Twenty-five years later, a famous conservationist named John Muir took interest in the region. He helped convince the U.S government to protect the forests and meadows surrounding Yosemite Valley, too. On October 1, 1890, the entire area became the United States' third national park.

National Park Fact File

A national park is land that is protected by the federal government. It is a place of importance to the United States because of its beauty, history, or value to scientists. The U.S. Congress creates a national park by passing a law. Here are some key facts about Yosemite National Park.

Yosemite National Park	
Location	Central California
Year established	1890
Size	1,169 square miles (3,028 sq km)
Average number of visitors each year	4 million
Height of the tallest waterfall	2,425 feet (739 meters), Yosemite Falls
Height of the tallest tree	210 feet (64 m), Grizzly Giant

People pose with a car on Overhanging Rock in 1916.

Rock Stars

Huge hunks of **granite** stand on each side of Yosemite Valley. These massive rock formations attract thousands of daring rock climbers and hikers each year. Some of the most famous rocks are Half Dome, Glacier Point, and El Capitan. Tourists are also drawn to the park's giant waterfalls, especially Yosemite Falls. Its total height of 2,425 feet (739 m) is taller than most of the tallest skyscrapers in the world!

In spring, about 135,000 gallons (511,031 liters) of water flow from Yosemite Falls every minute.

A Hair-Raising Hike

Half Dome is one of the park's biggest rock formations. It is about 4,800 feet (1,463 m) tall. Each year, thousands of people hike to its **summit**. The last 400 feet (122 m) is the hardest part. Hikers must climb straight up the side of the steep rock. They pull themselves up using two metal cables attached to the side of a cliff. Some people wear gloves so they do not lose their grip.

It takes about 10 to 12 hours to hike to the top of Half Dome and back.

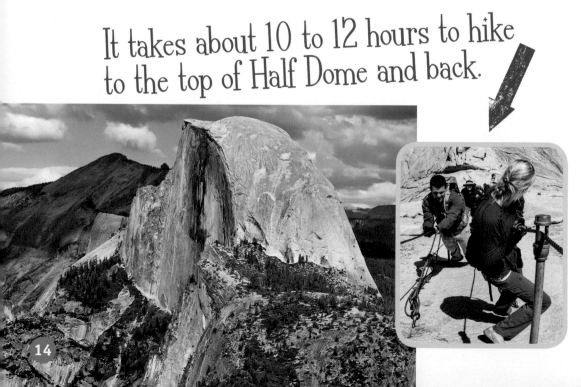

A couple dances on Overhanging Rock in the 1890s.

Deadly Drop

A popular place to take pictures is the Overhanging Rock. It is on Glacier Point, a rock formation that overlooks Yosemite Valley. Visitors have been posing on Overhanging Rock for more than 150 years. A few people have even done handstands on it. But tourists should think twice about going too close to the rock's edge. It is a very long way down to the ground: more than 3,000 feet (914 m)!

A climber clings to the side of El Capitan.

Top of the Rock

El Capitan is another gigantic rock formation in Yosemite. At more than 3,000 feet (914 m) above the valley floor, it is not the tallest formation in the park. But rock climbers say it is the toughest rock in the world to climb. Getting to the top of El Capitan is challenging because of its smooth, steep sides. There is not much to hold on to!

Don't Look Down

In January 2015, rock climbers Tommy Caldwell and Kevin Jorgeson made history. They became the first people to free-climb the Dawn Wall. This is the southeast face of El Capitan in Yosemite. The pair spent 19 days scaling the rock face using only their hands and feet. They slept in a portable tent called a portaledge, which can be attached to a rock face. They also had safety ropes to catch their falls.

Wild Waterfalls

Waterfalls seem to be everywhere in Yosemite. Each winter, snow covers Yosemite's mountaintops. When the weather warms up in the spring, the snow melts into water and floods the streams and creeks. The water flows down, then gushes over the park's rocky cliffs. The best time to see the waterfalls is during May and June. The rest of the year, the falls may slow to a trickle or even dry up completely.

Visitors peer down a waterfall from a viewing spot at the top of Vernal Fall.

Yosemite's Famous Falls

Yosemite has countless waterfalls. Here are some of the most breathtaking ones.

NAME	HEIGHT	FACT	
Park Waterfalls			
Bridalveil Falls	620 feet (189 m)	Bridalveil is the first waterfall visitors see when they enter the park.	
Horsetail Falls	1,575 feet (480 m)	Each February, if the weather and water flow are just right, sunlight hits this waterfall in a special way. It gives the flowing water a bright orange glow. People say the waterfall looks like it is on fire.	
Ribbon Falls	1,612 feet (491 m)	This waterfall has the highest single-drop in North America. It cascades down the cliff on the west side of El Capitan.	
Yosemite Falls	2,425 feet (739 m)	Yosemite Falls is made up of three sections. Its total height makes it the tallest waterfall in the United States and one of the tallest in North America.	

CHAPTER 3

Amazing Animals

If you go to Yosemite, pack binoculars. You might spot a black bear! About 500 of them live in Yosemite Valley. For decades, the park had feeding stations for the bears so visitors could see them up close. That ended in 1971 because the bears were coming too close for comfort! Today, park visitors must store their food in bear-proof containers. Locked cars and tents are not good places to keep food. Bears can easily get into them.

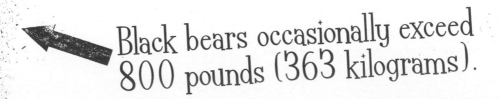

Black bears occasionally exceed 800 pounds (363 kilograms).

At Home in the Forest

Yosemite's forests are packed with wildlife. Many mammals, including bobcats and gray foxes, live in them. Nearly 20 species of bats, such as the western mastiff, roost in the forest. They usually hide out in caves and in the holes of trees. There are also mountain kingsnakes and rubber boas that slither through the fallen leaves. Great gray owls and golden eagles soar overhead.

More than half of all great gray owls in California live in Yosemite.

A pale swallowtail butterfly perches on a flower in Yosemite.

Down in the Meadow

More than 70 different types of butterflies flutter through Yosemite's meadows. They slurp the nectar from the many wildflowers there. The most common butterfly species are Sierra sulphur, the greenish blue, Edith's checkerspot, and orange sulphur.

Herds of mule deer can also be spotted in the fields, nibbling on the lush green grass. But beware! If deer are around, a mountain lion may be lurking nearby, hoping to catch one for dinner.

National Parks Field Guide:
Yosemite

Here are a few of the hundreds of fascinating animals you may see in the park.

Coyote

Scientific name: *Canis latrans*

Habitat: Meadows and valleys

Diet: Mainly rodents, such as mice and squirrels

Fact: Many people mistake coyotes for wolves. But there are no wolves in Yosemite.

Great gray owl

Scientific name: *Strix nebulosa*

Habitat: Nests are found where forests and meadows meet

Diet: Mainly rodents, such as voles

Fact: This big bird is the largest owl in North America. It is 2 feet (0.6 m) tall, with a 5-foot (1.5 m) wingspan.

American pika

Scientific name: *Ochotona princeps*

Habitat: Fields in mountainous areas

Diet: Grasses, thistles, and other green plants

Fact: Though it looks mouselike, its closest relative is the rabbit.

Sacramento sucker

Scientific name: *Catostomus occidentalis*

Habitat: Lower Merced and Tuolumne River systems

Diet: Algae, water insects, fish eggs

Fact: Fishermen use balls of dough to catch this greenish-brown fish.

Western pond turtle

Scientific name: *Actinemys marmorata*

Habitat: The Hetch Hetchy area in streams, pools, and vegetated banks

Diet: Insects, frog eggs, tadpoles, and snails

Fact: This reptile was reintroduced into Yosemite Valley in 2016 after an almost 50-year absence.

Pacific tree frog

Scientific name: *Pseudacris regilla*

Habitat: Throughout the park, especially in meadows and woodlands

Diet: Spiders, insects

Fact: Rock climbers have spotted this tiny amphibian hopping around on the rock walls of El Capitan. It lives in the cracks.

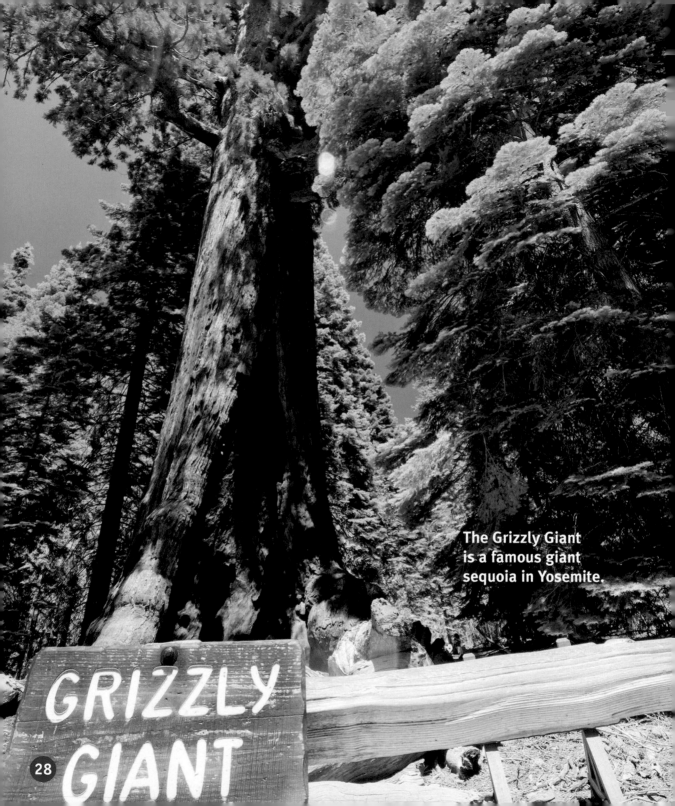

The Grizzly Giant is a famous giant sequoia in Yosemite.

GRIZZLY GIANT

CHAPTER 4

Towering Trees

Imagine a tree that is taller than the Statue of Liberty. That tree is real! It is called a giant sequoia. Giant sequoias are among the tallest trees in the world. They are so wide that people once cut tunnels through their trunks and drove cars through them. These huge trees are also among the planet's oldest living things. Some of the giant sequoias in Yosemite sprouted more than 2,000 years ago.

Giant sequoias grow naturally only in the Sierra Nevada mountain range of California.

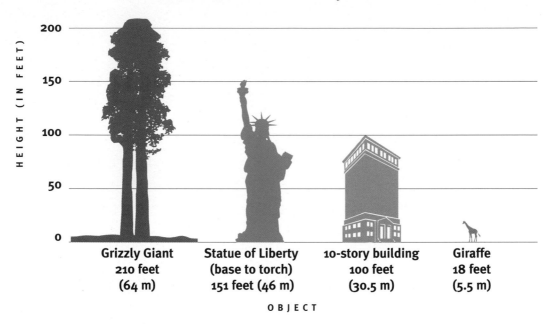

How Tall Is the Grizzly Giant?

HEIGHT (IN FEET)

Grizzly Giant	Statue of Liberty	10-story building	Giraffe
210 feet	(base to torch)	100 feet	18 feet
(64 m)	151 feet (46 m)	(30.5 m)	(5.5 m)

OBJECT

Grizzly Giant

The easiest place to see giant sequoias in Yosemite is in Mariposa Grove. About 500 of the trees can be found there. The most famous is called the Grizzly Giant. This tree is the largest giant sequoia in the park. It is 210 feet (64 m) tall! That's taller than two stacked ten-story buildings! These gigantic trees can also be found in Tuolumne Grove and Merced Grove.

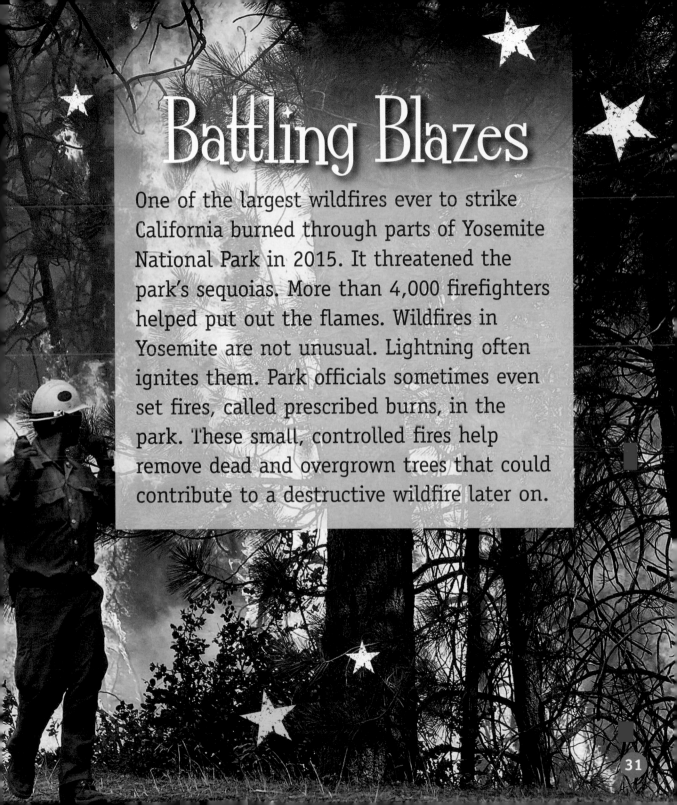

Battling Blazes

One of the largest wildfires ever to strike California burned through parts of Yosemite National Park in 2015. It threatened the park's sequoias. More than 4,000 firefighters helped put out the flames. Wildfires in Yosemite are not unusual. Lightning often ignites them. Park officials sometimes even set fires, called prescribed burns, in the park. These small, controlled fires help remove dead and overgrown trees that could contribute to a destructive wildfire later on.

Essential to Survival

Besides the giant sequoias, more than 1,500 species of plants grow in Yosemite. For much of their history, the native Ahwahneechee people depended on many of these plants to live. They used them for food, building materials, and medicine. The California black oak's acorns made up a big part of their diet. They used rocks to grind the nuts into flour to make bread, mush, and soup. The Ahwahneechee also used incense cedar and lodgepole pine to build everything from baskets to shelters.

Visit Yosemite in the fall to see the black oaks' leaves turn beautiful colors.

Yarrow grows in stalks with dense clusters of tiny flowers.

Other plants, including yarrow, yerba santa, and wormwood, provided medicine for the Ahwahneechee. They used these plants to help cure everything from headaches to snakebites. Leaves, flowers, and roots were ground down and boiled into a special tea. They were also mashed into a paste and applied to the skin to speed healing and prevent infection.

A climber makes his way to the top of Lost Arrow Spire.

CHAPTER 5

Protecting the Park

Yosemite is often called a national treasure. The National Park Service (NPS) works hard to keep it that way. That can be a challenge when about 4 million people visit the park each year. Increasing numbers of cars and buses have led to crumbling roads and overcrowded facilities. Visitors leave behind tons of trash as they pass through. Even some of the park's natural wonders, such as the giant sequoias, have been affected.

People throw out about 2,200 tons of garbage in Yosemite each year.

Traffic Trouble

Traffic is a growing problem in Yosemite. People can be stuck for up to two hours, especially on the weekends. To improve the traffic, the National Park Service began extensive road repairs in 2016.

Officials are also working to improve how traffic flows in and around the park.

Traffic at Yosemite

Average Monthly Visitation

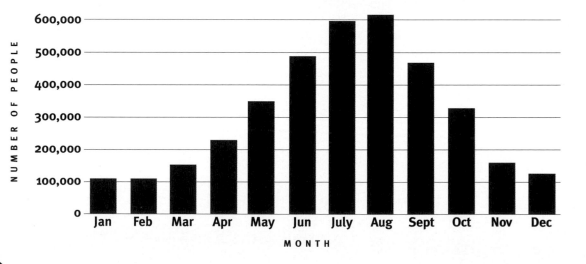

NUMBER OF PEOPLE

MONTH

A visitor stops to enjoy the sequoias in Mariposa Grove.

Saving Sequoias

Over time, the park's heavy visitor traffic posed a threat to the giant sequoias. The tree roots were being trampled and driven over. Damaged roots can cause trees to topple. To protect them, park officials carried out a major **restoration** beginning in 2014. Park officials removed a parking lot and a gift shop that had been built over some trees' roots. These structures were replaced with a special walkway over the roots.

37

A rockfall severely damaged trees and a cabin in the park in 2008.

On Shaky Ground

Other threats to Yosemite are natural ones. They include small earthquakes, heavy rainstorms, and **erosion**. All three can cause rockfalls. These are fast, massive movements of rocks down a cliff, mountain, or other formation. Over the past 150 years, there have been more than 1,000 rockfalls. They can put tourists, especially rock climbers, in danger. **Geologists** monitor rockfall events. They work with park officials to keep people out of harm's way.

Planning for the Future

The National Park Service continues to expand and conserve Yosemite National Park. In 2016, an area equal to 400 acres (162 hectares) was added to the park's almost 750,000-acre (303,514 ha) total. It includes a **wetlands** habitat and a grassy meadow surrounded by a pine and fir forest. Park officials hope that new areas such as this one will give wildlife more space to thrive. They will also give future generations of visitors more room to roam. ★

Wildflowers bloom in Ackerson Meadow, which became part of Yosemite National Park in 2016.

Map Mystery

What famous Yosemite attraction is known as Tu-Tok-A-Nu'-La by the Ahwahneechee? Follow the directions below to find the answer.

Directions

1. Start at the Tioga Pass Entrance.

2. Go south to Mount Lyell, Yosemite's highest point.

3. Travel southwest to Mariposa Grove, home of the Grizzly Giant.

4. You're almost there! Head north toward Yosemite Valley.

5. Look for the giant rock formation between Ribbon Falls and Horsetail Falls. Its name is the answer.

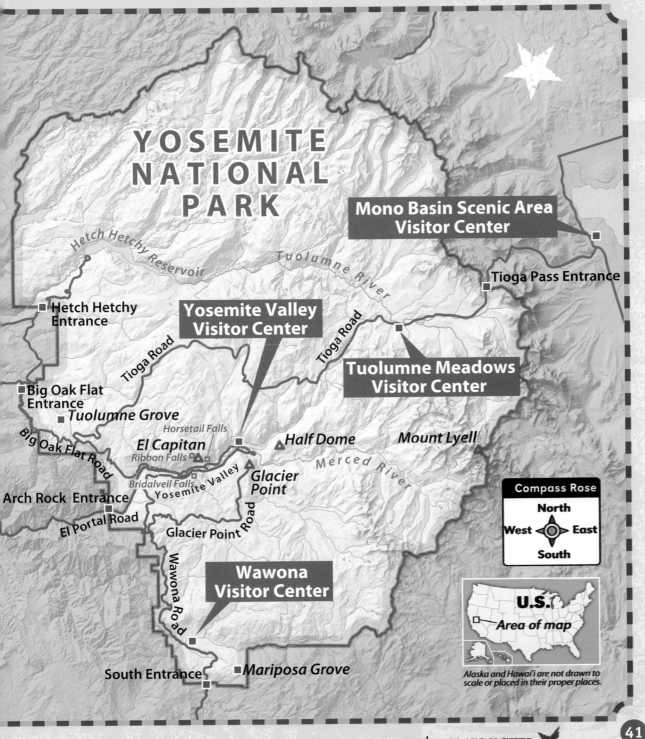

YOSEMITE NATIONAL PARK

Mono Basin Scenic Area Visitor Center

Hetch Hetchy Reservoir

Tuolumne River

Tioga Pass Entrance

Hetch Hetchy Entrance

Yosemite Valley Visitor Center

Tioga Road

Tioga Road

Tuolumne Meadows Visitor Center

Big Oak Flat Entrance

Tuolumne Grove

Big Oak Flat Road

Horsetail Falls

El Capitan

Ribbon Falls

Half Dome

Mount Lyell

Merced River

Bridalveil Falls

Yosemite Valley

Glacier Point

Arch Rock Entrance

El Portal Road

Glacier Point Road

Compass Rose

North

West ← → East

South

Wawona Visitor Center

Wawona Road

U.S.

→ Area of map

Alaska and Hawai'i are not drawn to scale or placed in their proper places.

South Entrance

Mariposa Grove

★ **Answer:** El Capitan

41

Be an Animal Tracker!

If you're ever in Yosemite, keep an eye out for these animal tracks. They'll help you know which animals are in the area.

Bighorn sheep
Hoof length: 3 inches (8 cm)

Bobcat
Paw length: 2 inches (5 cm)

Black bear

Paw length: 3.5 to 5 inches (9 to 13 cm)

Coyote

Paw length: 2.5 inches (6 cm)

Mule deer

Hoof length: 3 inches (8 cm)

Yellow-bellied marmot

Paw length: 1.5 inches (4 cm)

True Statistics

Average snowfall: 29 in. (74 cm)

Species of trees: 35

Number of black bears: About 500

Amount of garbage thrown away each year: About 2,200 tons

Number of mammal species in the park: About 90

Number of bird species: 262

Number of amphibian species: 12, including 11 native and 1 non-native

Number of reptile species: 22

Number of insect and other arthropod species: Thousands

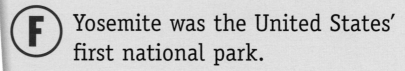

Did you find the truth?

F Yosemite was the United States' first national park.

T Some trees in Yosemite are more than 2,000 years old.

GRIZZLY GIANT

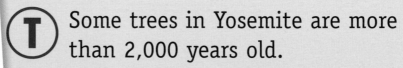

Resources

Books

Flynn, Sarah Wassner, and Julie Beer. *National Parks Guide U.S.A.* Washington, DC: National Geographic, 2016.

Graf, Mike. *My Yosemite: A Guide for Young Adventurers.* Berkeley, CA: Heyday, 2012.

Ross, Michael Elsohn. *Yosemite Trivia.* Helena, MT: Riverbend Publishing, 2011.

Visit this Scholastic website for more information on Yosemite National Park:
★ www.factsfornow.scholastic.com
Enter the keyword **Yosemite**

Important Words

alpine (AL-pine) having to do with mountains

conservationists (kahn-sur-VAY-shuhn-ists) people who work to protect valuable things, especially forests, wildlife, natural resources, or artistic or historical objects

erosion (i-ROH-zhuhn) the wearing away of something by water or wind

geologists (jee-AH-luh-jists) people who study Earth's physical structure, especially its layers of soil and rock

glaciers (GLAY-shurz) slow-moving masses of ice found in mountain valleys or polar regions

granite (GRAN-it) a hard, gray rock often used in construction

groves (GROHVS) groups of trees growing or planted near one another

remote (ri-MOHT) far away; secluded or isolated

restoration (res-tuh-RAY-shuhn) the process of returning something to its original condition

summit (SUHM-it) the highest point of a mountain

wetlands (WET-landz) land where there is a lot of moisture in the soil

Index

Page numbers in **bold** indicate illustrations.

About the Author

Audra Wallace graduated from Ithaca College, where she studied film production and elementary education. Her passion for writing nonfiction and teaching kids led her to a position with Scholastic. Since 2006, Wallace has written and edited the award-winning classroom magazine *Scholastic News* Edition 3. She and her family enjoy exploring the great outdoors near their home in New York—and beyond!